To my sweet and funny son; my
adventurous and inspiring daughter; and
my supportive and handsome husband.
You encourage me to be better every day.

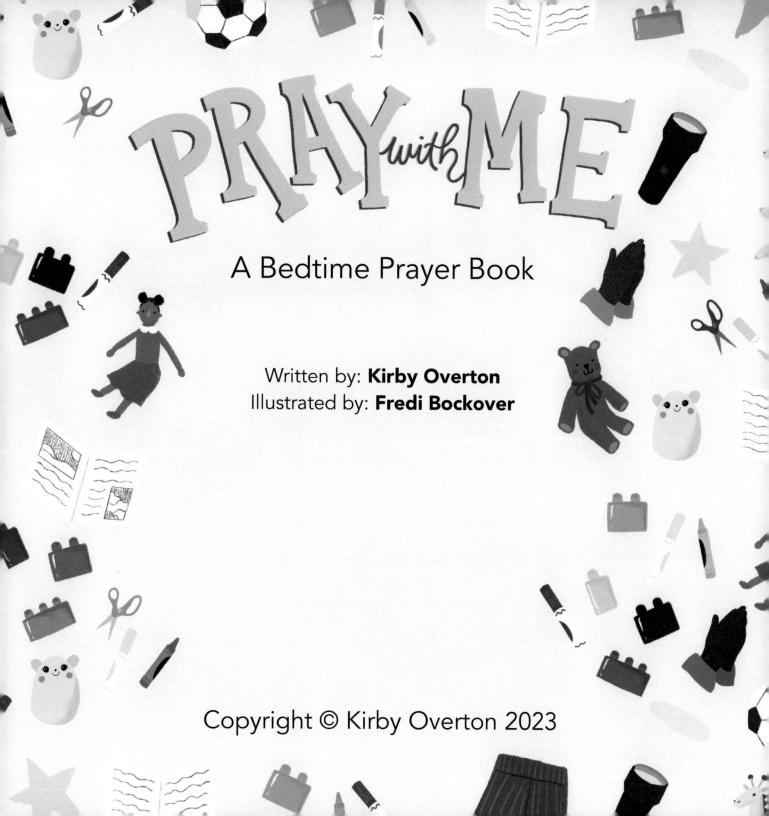

PRAY with ME

A Bedtime Prayer Book

Written by: **Kirby Overton**
Illustrated by: **Fredi Bockover**

Our day was full. We did our best.
It's night time now. We need our rest.

But before we lay our heads,
Let's say our prayers then go to bed.

Thank you, Lord, for blessing me,
Another day you let me see.

Thank you for my family,
My friends, my home, and community.

Thank you for my mom and dad,
Even when they make me mad.

Thank you for this wonderful day,
And for all the things I did not say.

Please protect us as we rest,
Lord, we know that we are blessed.

Tomorrow is another day,
I trust that you will guide my way.
Amen.

Goodnight mom and goodnight dad,
What a long day I have had.

Lots of playing and learning too,
I need my rest; there's more to do!

As I sleep I'll get strong and grow,
And in the morning I'll be ready to go!

Now it's time to go to sleep,
From me you won't hear another peep.

The Overton Family

_____**'s**

write your name here

Bedtime Prayers

This is me!

I am ____ years old.

My favorite color is
_____.

When I grow up, I
want to be

_____

_____.

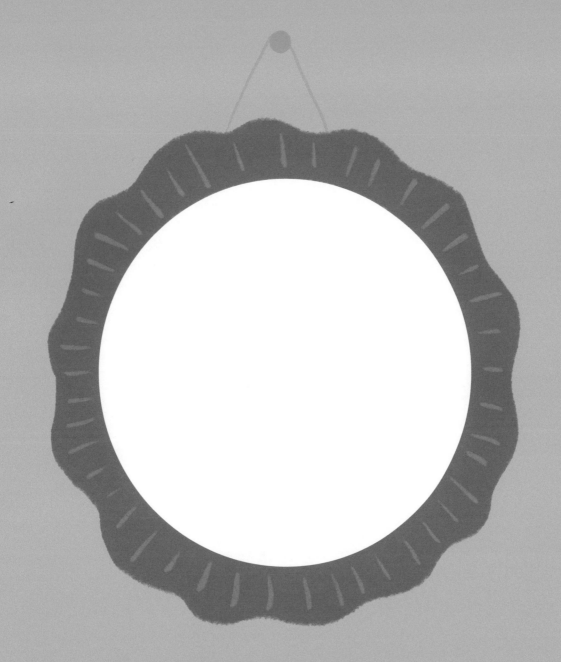

This is my family.
I am grateful for them because they are

_____.

This is what my
bed looks like.

This is my favorite
stuffed animal. I can't
go to sleep without it!

This is what my favorite pajamas look like. They are
_____.

I got them from
_____.

What I'm Grateful For

Who I Want to Pray For